The Sayi

The Sayings of

GEORGE
ORWELL

edited by
Robert Pearce

Duckworth

First published in 1994 by
Gerald Duckworth & Co. Ltd.
The Old Piano Factory
48 Hoxton Square, London N1 6PB
Tel: 071 729 5986
Fax: 071 729 0015

A catalogue record for this book is available
from the British Library

ISBN 0 7156 2628 0

Typeset by Ray Davies
Printed in Great Britain by
Redwood Books, Trowbridge

Contents

Introduction

Eric Blair wrote his first poem at the age of four or five, about a tiger with 'chair-like teeth', and at the age of eleven one of his works was published. An introspective and somewhat solitary boy, in whose mind stories formed almost involuntarily, he seemed a born writer. He made no secret that he was to be not merely a writer but a 'FAMOUS WRITER'. Yet to the man, such ambitions seemed childish things to be put away. After leaving Eton, where he had won a scholarship from St Cyprian's in Eastbourne, he followed his father by taking up a position in the British Empire, and from 1922 to 1927 he served as a policeman in Burma. But nagging doubts remained. Was he not somehow violating his real nature? He decided to throw up his safe but uncongenial career and earn his living as a writer. He had chosen a very precarious existence. His first novels were destroyed, after publishers' rejections, and he was earning more from odd jobs – from tutoring and washing-up – than from writing. The only way to make money from writing, he later quipped, is to marry a publisher's daughter. Then, in 1933, *Down and Out in Paris and London* was published and 'George Orwell' – mercifully preferred as a pseudonym to 'H. Lewis Allways' – was born.

Success came slowly, and writing still had to be combined with more regularly-paid occupations. Yet *Down and Out* was followed by four novels – *Burmese Days, A Clergyman's Daughter, Keep the Aspidistra Flying* and *Coming Up For Air* – and by two works retailing his experiences in the north of England and Spain, *The Road to Wigan Pier* and *Homage to Catalonia*. He also proved himself an able essayist and journalist. But it was with the publication of *Animal Farm*, in 1945, and *Nineteen Eighty-Four*, in 1949, that Orwell was recognised as an indubitably great writer.

Was there a more dedicated writer than Orwell until his death from tuberculosis at the age of forty-six? He seems to have been driven to write, so that, in his own words, 'there has literally not been one day in which I did not feel that I was idling, that I was behind with the current job, and that my total output was miserably small'. In fact, his output was prodigious. In hospital towards the end of his life, when his right arm was put in plaster, he quickly learned to write with his left hand. Those who knew him would have expected no less. Only death could stop him.

Yet he was no study-bound scribbler: instead, he wrote out of first-hand experience, generally painful. He lived the life of a 'down and out'; he stayed with miners in Wigan; he fought – and very nearly died – in the Spanish Civil War; and the Ministry of Truth, in *Nineteen Eighty-Four*, was to some extent modelled on the BBC, where he worked for a time during the Second World War. No writer drew more on the bedrock of his own memory, and no writer can have cared so much about his work and so little about his health.

Above all, Orwell is remembered for making political writing into an art. He saw things incorrigibly in political terms. His school friend Cyril Connolly once said that he could not blow his nose without moralising on conditions in the handkerchief industry. He called himself a convinced socialist, remarking that after 1936 every serious word he wrote had been written '*against* totalitarianism and *for* democratic Socialism, as I understand it'. But those last four words were necessary, for he was no orthodox socialist. He was too much the individualist and outsider for that: no man was less likely to toe any prescribed political line or more inclined to castigate the 'smelly little orthodoxies' contending for our souls. Nor was he by temperament a political animal. He once speculated that, in different times, he might have been a happy vicar, content 'To preach upon eternal doom / And watch my walnuts grow'. Instead, he faced the harsh truths of the era of Hitler and Stalin with clear-sighted awareness. Even so, his mind was never dominated by politics, and his writings reveal a remarkable range of interests. Only music and abstract philosophy seemed to fall outside his intellectual span. He was, to use his own term, an 'elastic brow'.

He did not, however, possess an elastic conscience. Indeed most writers have praised him as a scrupulously honest person, as a man who 'fought a duel against lies', mobilising the English language in the process. There can be no doubt that, after a long apprenticeship of unceasing effort, he made himself into a brilliant prose stylist, the fiercest opponent of cant, jargon and mystification. He believed that what can be said can be said clearly, and with freshness and elegance as well. But he was also a *provocative* writer, challenging readers to think for themselves rather than tamely accept what they were told, even by him. He knew that everyone was biased, including himself, and he urged us all to be on our guard. With good reason. In speech he had a habit of outrageous generalisation: 'All tobacconists are fascists', he once said, while 'All scoutmasters are homosexuals'. A few weeks before his death he was arguing that judges wanted to keep the death penalty because of the erotic satisfaction they derived from a hanging. This was a man who clearly enjoyed ideas, sometimes perverse ones. He always tried to tell the truth, but by this he sometimes meant being true to his feelings rather than to mere facts, and at times he could be uncharitable. 'Little fat men' seemed to earn his wrath merely by being little and fat, especially if they inclined towards baldness and had vegetarian or teetotal leanings. Orwell, of course, was tall and thin, with a thick head of hair, a meat-eater and beer-drinker.

Orwell is often depicted as the sort of pessimist who makes Thomas Hardy appear a blithe spirit. The good end unhappily: that is what Orwellian fiction means. In his earliest novel, *Burmese Days*, John Flory committed suicide, while in his last, *Nineteen Eighty-Four*, the ending is even more hopeless: Winston Smith, after the horrors of Room 101, ended by loving Big Brother. The Publisher's Report on this final work described it as 'amongst the most terrifying books I have ever read. The savagery of Swift has passed to a successor who looks upon life and finds it becoming ever more intolerable'. Characteristically, his first recorded word as a baby had been 'beastly'!

I do not wish to argue that Orwell was not temperamentally inclined to look on the dark side of life and, at times, to deny that a bright side existed. He was indeed, as V.S. Pritchett described him, the *'wintry* conscience of a generation'. *Pessimism* contains more quotations than any other section in this book, and this courageous man, who could face any adversity, sometimes flinched when presented with good news. But there is much more to Orwell than horror and gloom. Like Camus' Sisyphus, surmounting his fate by scorn, he was sometimes able to conclude that all is well. He was not so pessimistic as to stop fighting against cruelty and lies. *Nineteen Eighty-Four*, after all, was a warning not a prediction. He also cared passionately about literature and prose style; he loved nature and the 'surface of the earth', taking pleasure in 'solid objects' as well as 'scraps of useless information'. He was also a profound, though critical, patriot. His recognition that suffering is a large part of every human life enabled him to value all the more the genuine satisfactions that come our way. This pious unbeliever had a contempt for 'shallow, gutless hedonism' as a philosophy of life but not for all pleasure. 'Orwellian' will never mean light-hearted or funny; but it is too seldom recognised that Orwell had high regard for humour and could be witty and sometimes brilliantly comic as well as sardonic.

Orwell was a many-minded man. He was Eric Blair as well as George Orwell. Certainly he was often emotionally attracted to what he intellectually rejected and, similarly, repelled by what he consciously approved. He felt that there was something appealing in Hitler, just as he recognised value in the British Raj which he hated. In consequence, the range of his sayings, as illustrated in the following selection, is remarkably diverse. He would have been the first to deny the title of 'sage', just as he would have battled fiercely against the sainthood that some have posthumously awarded him: but there is wit and wisdom, as well as verbal brilliance and inspired common sense in all his writings. There is also 'decency', the quality he admired so much. He remains one of the most courageous, original and compelling writers of the twentieth century – and one who will continue to inspire, terrify and occasionally infuriate into the twenty-first.

R.D.P.

Sources

Works by Orwell

Down and Out in Paris and London (1933)
Burmese Days (1934)
A Clergyman's Daughter (1935)
Keep the Aspidistra Flying (1936)
The Road to Wigan Pier (1937)
Homage to Catalonia (1938)
Coming Up For Air (1939)
Inside the Whale (1940)
The Lion and the Unicorn (1941)
Animal Farm (1945)
Critical Essays (1946)
The English People (1947)
Nineteen Eighty-Four (1949)
Shooting an Elephant (1950)
Such, Such Were the Joys (1953)
Collected Essays (1961)
The Collected Essays, Journalism and Letters of George Orwell, 4 volumes (1968)
George Orwell: The War Broadcasts (1985)
George Orwell: The War Commentaries (1985)

Other sources

Bernard Crick, *George Orwell: A Life* (1980)
Michael Shelden, *Orwell: The Authorised Biography* (1991)

Poverty & Wealth

A man who has gone even a week on bread and margarine is not a man any longer, only a belly with a few accessory organs.

Down and Out in Paris and London

It is fatal to look hungry. It makes people want to kick you.   *ibid.*

You have talked so often of going to the dogs – and well, here are the dogs, and you have reached them, and you can stand it. It takes off a lot of anxiety.

ibid.

The waiter ... has the pleasure of spending money by proxy.

ibid.

It is not a figure of speech, it is a mere statement of fact to say that a French cook will spit in the soup – that is, if he is not going to drink it himself. He is an artist, but his art is not cleanliness.   *ibid.*

Roughly speaking, the more one pays for food, the more sweat and spittle one is obliged to eat with it.

ibid.

Essentially, a 'smart' hotel is a place where a hundred people toil like devils in order that two hundred may pay through the nose for things they do not really want.
ibid.

The mass of the rich and the poor are differentiated by their incomes and nothing else, and the average millionaire is only the average dishwasher dressed in a new suit. Change places, and handy dandy, which is the justice, which is the thief?

ibid.

Dirt is a great respecter of persons; it lets you alone when you are well dressed, but as soon as your collar is gone it flies towards you from all directions.

ibid.

A navvy works by swinging a pick. An accountant works by adding up figures. A beggar works by standing out of doors in all weathers and getting varicose veins ... He is honest compared with the sellers of most patent medicines, high-minded compared with a Sunday newspaper proprietor, amiable compared with a hire-purchase tout – in short, a parasite, but a fairly harmless parasite.

ibid.

Money has become the grand test of virtue. By this test beggars fail, and for this they are despised. If one could earn even ten pounds a week at begging, it would become a respectable profession immediately.

ibid.

It is curious how people take it for granted that they have a right to preach at you and pray over you as soon as your income falls below a certain level.

ibid.

A man receiving charity practically always hates his benefactor – it is a fixed characteristic of human nature.

ibid.

I shall never again think that all tramps are drunken scoundrels, nor expect a begger to be grateful when I give him a penny, nor be surprised if men out of work lack energy, nor subscribe to the Salvation Army, nor pawn my clothes, nor refuse a handbill, nor enjoy a meal at a smart restaurant.

ibid.

The first effect of poverty is that it kills thought.

Keep the Aspidistra Flying

Mental deadness, spiritual squalor – they seem to descend upon you when your income drops below a certain point.

ibid.

Faith, hope, money – only a saint could have the first two without having the third.

ibid.

How many girls alive wouldn't be manless sooner than take on a man who's moneyless?

ibid.

No rich man ever succeeds in disguising himself as a poor man; for money, like murder, will out.

ibid.

The fatty degeneration of the spirit that goes with wealth.
ibid.

Poverty is spiritual halitosis.

ibid.

You can possess money, or you can despise money; the only fatal thing is to worship money and fail to get it.
ibid.

Dirt is a thing people make too much fuss about. It is astonishing how quickly you get used to doing without a handkerchief and to eating out of the tin pannikin in which you also wash.

Homage to Catalonia

People with empty bellies never despair of the universe.
Collected Essays, Journalism and Letters, vol. 1

A human being is primarily a bag for putting food into; the other functions and faculties may be more godlike, but in point of time they come afterwards.
The Road to Wigan Pier

When you are unemployed, which is to say when you are underfed, harassed, bored and miserable, you don't want to eat dull wholesome food. You want something a little bit 'tasty'.

ibid.

Tramps ... have nothing worthy to be called conversation, because emptiness of belly leaves no speculation in their souls ... Their next meal is never quite secure, and so they cannot think of anything except the next meal.

Collected Essays, Journalism and Letters, vol. 1

I should like to see clothes rationing continue till the moths have devoured the last dinner-jacket ... If the poor are not much better dressed, at least the rich are shabbier.

ibid., vol. 3

The English & Foreigners

There will be no revolution in England while there are aspidistras in the windows.

Keep the Aspidistra Flying

The English will never develop into a nation of philosophers. They will always prefer instinct to logic, and character to intelligence. But they must get rid of their downright contempt for 'cleverness'. They cannot afford it any longer.

Collected Essays, Journalism and Letters, vol. 3

Most English people are constitutionally incapable of believing that anything will ever change.

ibid., vol. 1

Nowadays there is no mob only a flock.   *ibid.*

In England, for mainly geographical reasons, sport, especially field-sports, and snobbery are inextricably mingled.   *ibid.*

What can the England of 1940 have in common with the England of 1840? But then, what have you in common with the child of five whose photograph your mother keeps on the mantelpiece? Nothing, except that you happen to be the same person.

The Lion and the Unicorn

At bottom it is the same quality in the English character that repels the tourist and keeps out the invader.   *ibid.*

In England such concepts as justice, liberty and objective truth are still believed in.   *ibid.*

England is the most class-ridden country under the sun. It is a land of snobbery and privilege, ruled largely by the old and silly.   *ibid.*

When you come back to England from any foreign country, you have immediately the sensation of breathing a different air ... The beer is bitterer, the coins are heavier, the grass is greener, the advertisements are more blatant. *ibid.*

Talk to foreigners, read foreign books or newspapers, and you are immediately brought back to the same thought. Yes, there is something distinctive and recognizable in English civilization.

ibid.

A family with the wrong members in control – that, perhaps, is as near as one can come to describing England in a phrase. *ibid.*

The gentleness of English civilization is perhaps its most marked characteristic ... In no country inhabited by white men is it easier to shove people off the pavement.
ibid.

Probably the battle of Waterloo *was* won on the playing-fields of Eton, but the opening battles of all subsequent wars have been lost there. One of the dominant facts in English life during the last three quarters of a century has been the decay of ability in the ruling class. *ibid.*

In left-wing circles it is always felt that there is something slightly disgraceful in being an Englishman and that it is a duty to snigger at every English institution, from horse racing to suet puddings. It is a strange fact, but it is unquestionably true that any English intellectual would feel more ashamed of standing to attention during 'God save the King' than of stealing from a poor box.

ibid.

The heirs of Nelson and Cromwell are not in the House of Lords. They are in the fields and the streets, in the factories and the armed forces, in the four-ale bar and the suburban back garden.

ibid.

Nothing ever stands still. We must add to our heritage or lose it, we must grow greater or grow less, we must go forward or backward. I believe in England, and I believe that we shall go forward. *ibid.*

In a country like England you can no more be cultured without money than you can join the Cavalry Club.
Keep the Aspidistra Flying

Not merely a hatred of bullying, but a tendency to support the weaker side merely because it is weaker, are almost general in England.
Collected Essays, Journalism and Letters, vol. 3

The English are not sufficiently interested in intellectual matters to be intolerant of them.
ibid.

The outstanding and – by contemporary standards – highly original quality of the English is their habit of *not killing one another*. *ibid.*

Earthquakes in Japan, famines in China, revolutions in Mexico? Don't worry, the milk will be on the doorstep tomorrow morning, and the *New Statesman* will come out on Friday. *Homage to Catalonia*

The world is sick of chaos and it is sick of dictatorship. Of all peoples the English are likeliest to find a way of avoiding both.
Collected Essays, Journalism and Letters, vol. 3

The English regional snobberies are nationalism in miniature. *The Road to Wigan Pier*

There can hardly be a town in the South of England where you could throw a brick without hitting the niece of a bishop. *ibid.*

During the past dozen years the English working class have grown servile with a rather horrifying rapidity.
ibid.

There is no *turbulence* left in England.
> *Collected Essays, Journalism and Letters*, vol. 1

What the majority of English people mean by an apple is a lump of highly-coloured cotton wool from America or Australia.
> *The Road to Wigan Pier*

The Americans always go one better in any kind of beastliness, whether it is ice-cream soda, racketeering or theosophy.
> *Keep the Aspidistra Flying*

Why is it that the worst extremes of jingoism and racialism have to be tolerated when they come from an Irishman?
> *Collected Essays, Journalism and Letters*, vol. 4

Considering what the history of Anglo-Irish relations has been, it is not surprising that there should be Irishmen whose life-work is abusing England: what does call for remark is that they should be able to look to the English public for support.
> *ibid.*

I defy anyone to be thrown as I was among the Spanish working class ... and not be struck by their essential decency; above all, their straightforwardness and generosity.
> *Homage to Catalonia*

The Spaniards are good at many things, but not at making war.
> *ibid.*

In Spain nothing, from a meal to a battle, ever happens at the appointed time.
> *ibid.*

Religion

In theory it is still possible to be an orthodox religious believer without being intellectually crippled in the process; but it is far from easy.

Collected Essays, Journalism and Letters, vol. 2

If death ends everything, it becomes much harder to believe that you can be in the right even if you are defeated.

ibid., vol. 3

The real problem is how to restore the religious attitude while accepting death as final. Men can only be happy when they do not assume that the object of life is happiness.

ibid.

I have always thought there might be a lot of cash in starting a new religion.

ibid., vol. 1

Saints should always be judged guilty until they are proved innocent.

ibid., vol. 4

No doubt alcohol, tobacco and so forth are things that a saint must avoid, but sainthood is also a thing that human beings must avoid.

ibid.

Many people genuinely do not wish to be saints, and it is probable that some who achieve or aspire to sainthood have never felt much temptation to be human beings.

ibid.

The Catholic and the Communist are alike in assuming that an opponent cannot be both honest and intelligent.

ibid.

One cannot really be Catholic and grown-up.

ibid.

He was an embittered atheist (the sort of atheist who does not so much disbelieve in God as personally dislike Him).

Down and Out in Paris and London

... the Prayer Book, which I have been studying for some days past in hopes of steeling myself against the obscenities of the wedding service.

Collected Essays, Journalism and Letters, vol. 1

Money is what God used to be. Good and evil have no meaning any longer except success and failure.

Keep the Aspidistra Flying

It is a fact – you have only to look about you to verify it – that the pious and the immoral drift naturally together. The best brothel-scenes in literature have been written, without exception, by pious believers or pious unbelievers.

A Clergyman's Daughter

Man is not an individual, he is only a cell in an everlasting body, and he is dimly aware of it.

Collected Essays, Journalism and Letters, vol. 2

Faith vanishes but the need for faith remains the same as before.

A Clergyman's Daughter

Politics & War

The fact is that you cannot help living in the manner appropriate and developing the ideology appropriate to your income.

Collected Essays, Journalism and Letters, vol. 1

I do not believe that a man with £50,000 a year and a man with fifteen shillings a week either can, or will, co-operate.

ibid.

Whereas the bourgeois goes through life expecting to get what he wants, within limits, the working man always feels himself the slave of a more or less mysterious authority.

ibid.

Nine times out of ten a revolutionary is merely a climber with a bomb in his pocket.

ibid.

Patriotism has nothing to do with conservatism. It is devotion to something that is changing but is felt to be mystically the same.

ibid.

To survive you often have to fight, and to fight you have to dirty yourself. War is evil, and it is often the lesser evil.

ibid., vol. 2

Whether the British ruling class are wicked or merely stupid is one of the most difficult questions of our time.

ibid.

How right the working class are in their 'materialism'! How right they are to realize that the belly comes before the soul, not in the scale of values but in point of time!

ibid.

In power politics there are no crimes, because there are no laws. *ibid.*

People took politics seriously in those days. They used to begin storing up rotten eggs weeks before an election.
Coming Up For Air

[Parody of Russian show-trials]
Almost every day some dastardly act of sabotage is laid bare – sometimes a plot to blow up the House of Lords, sometimes an outbreak of foot and mouth disease in the Royal racing-stables. Eighty per cent of Beefeaters at the Tower are discovered to be agents of the Comintern. A high official at the Post Office admits brazenly to having embezzled postal orders to the tune of £5,000,000 and also to having committed *lèse majesté* by drawing moustaches on postage stamps.
Collected Essays, Journalism and Letters, vol. 1

A thousand influences constantly press a working man down into a *passive* role. He does not act, he is acted on.
The Road to Wigan Pier

The real enemies of the working class are not those who talk to them in a too highbrow manner; they are those who try to trick them into identifying their interests with those of their exploiters.
Collected Essays, Journalism and Letters, vol. 1

Advertising is the dirtiest ramp that capitalism has yet invented.
Keep the Aspidistra Flying

The public are swine; advertising is the rattling of a stick inside a swill-bucket.
ibid.

The Communist and the Catholic are not saying the same thing, in a sense they are even saying the opposite things, and each would gladly boil the other in oil if circumstances permitted; but from the point of view of an outsider they are very much alike.
The Road to Wigan Pier

Every revolutionary opinion draws part of its strength from the conviction that nothing can be changed.

ibid.

The Great War ... could never have happened if tinned food had not been invented.

ibid.

Bugs are bad, but a state of affairs in which men will allow themselves to be dipped like sheep is worse.

ibid.

I sometimes believe that the price of liberty is not so much eternal vigilance as eternal dirt.

ibid.

It is quite likely that fish-and-chips, art-silk stockings, tinned salmon, cut-price chocolate (five two-ounce bars for sixpence), the movies, the radio, strong tea, and the Football Pools have between them averted revolution.

ibid.

It was said of these bombs that they were 'impartial'; they killed the man they were thrown at and the man who threw them.

Homage to Catalonia

Perhaps when the next great war comes we may see that sight unprecedented in all history, a jingo with a bullet-hole in him.

ibid.

'Realism' (it used to be called dishonesty) is part of the general political atmosphere of our time.

Collected Essays, Journalism and Letters, vol. 2

War is simply a reversal of civilized life; its motto is 'Evil be thou my good', and so much of modern life is actually evil that it is questionable whether on balance war does harm.

ibid.

Is it not a strange commentary on our time that ... the casualties in the present war cannot be estimated within several millions?

ibid., vol. 3

No one is patriotic about taxes.   *ibid.*, vol. 2

All propaganda is lies, even when one is telling the truth.
                                                    ibid.

What I like best is the careful grading by which the
honours are always dished out in direct proportion to
the amount of mischief done – baronies for Big Business,
baronetcies for fashionable surgeons, knighthoods for
tame professors.   *ibid.*, vol. 3

Everywhere able men feel themselves bottled down by
incompetent idiots from the county families.
                                                    ibid., vol. 2

During the years of investment capitalism we produced
like a belt of fat the huge blimpocracy which
monopolizes official and military power and has an
instinctive hatred of intelligence.
                                                    ibid.

You may not understand this, but I don't think it matters
killing people so long as you do not hate them.
                                                    ibid., vol. 3

Perhaps some degree of suffering is ineradicable from
human life, perhaps the choice before man is always the
choice of evils, perhaps even the aim of Socialism is not
to make the world perfect but to make it better. All
revolutions are failures, but they are not the same failure.
                                                    ibid.

It cannot be altogether an accident that nationalists of
the more extreme and romantic kind tend not to belong
to the nation that they idealize.
                                                    ibid.

The quickest way of ending a war is to lose it.
                                                    ibid., vol. 4

It is movements that make leaders and not leaders
movements.
                                                    The Lion and the Unicorn

No real revolutionary has ever been an internationalist.

ibid.

The mass of the people never get the chance to bring
their innate decency into the control of affairs, so that
one is almost driven to the cynical thought that men are
only decent when they are powerless.

Collected Essays, Journalism and Letters, vol. 1

Modern war is a racket.   *ibid.*

War is the greatest of all agents of change. It speeds up
all processes, wipes out minor distinctions, brings
realities to the surface. Above all, war brings it home to
the individual that he is *not* altogether an individual. It is
only because they are aware of this that men will die on
the field of battle.

The Lion and the Unicorn

People who in a normal way would have gone through
life with about as much tendency to think for themselves
as a suet pudding were turned into Bolshies just by the
war.

Coming Up For Air

If the war didn't happen to kill you it was bound to start
you thinking. After that unspeakable idiotic mess you
couldn't go on regarding society as something eternal
and unquestionable, like a pyramid. You knew it was
just a balls-up.

ibid.

One has to belong to the intelligentsia to believe things
like that: no ordinary man could be such a fool.

Collected Essays, Journalism and Letters, vol. 3

Man is the only creature that consumes without
producing.

Animal Farm

Napoleon had commanded that once a week there
should be held something called a Spontaneous
Demonstration.   *ibid.*

He adopted the maxim, 'Napoleon is always right', in addition to his private motto of 'I will work harder'.

ibid.

Four legs good, two legs bad.

ibid.

ALL ANIMALS ARE EQUAL
BUT SOME ANIMALS ARE MORE
EQUAL THAN OTHERS.

ibid.

The creatures outside looked from pig to man, and from man to pig, and from pig to man again; but already it was impossible to say which was which.

ibid.

The Two Minutes Hate

Nineteen Eighty-Four

Orthodoxy means not thinking – not needing to think. Orthodoxy means unconsciousness.

ibid.

Doublethink means the power of holding two contradictory beliefs in one's mind simultaneously, and accepting both of them.

ibid.

The secret of rulership is to combine a belief in one's own infallibility with the power to learn from past mistakes.

ibid.

On the battlefield, in the torture chamber, on a sinking ship, the issues that you are fighting for are always forgotten, because the body swells up until it fills the universe, and even when you are not paralysed by fright or screaming with pain, life is a moment-to-moment struggle against hunger or cold or sleeplessness, against a sour stomach or an aching tooth.

ibid.

The Proles, usually apathetic about war, were being
lashed into one of their periodic frenzies of patriotism.

ibid.

In the face of pain, there are no heroes.

ibid.

BIG BROTHER IS WATCHING YOU.

ibid.

One does not establish a dictatorship in order to
safeguard a revolution; one makes the revolution in
order to establish the dictatorship. The object of
persecution is persecution. The object of torture is
torture. The object of power is power.

ibid.

Man ... is an animal that can act morally when he acts as
an individual, but becomes unmoral when he acts
collectively.

Collected Essays, Journalism and Letters, vol. 4

The more one is aware of political bias the more one can
be independent of it, and the more one claims to be
impartial the more one is biassed.

ibid.

If liberty means anything at all it means the right to tell
people what they do not want to hear.

Michael Shelden, *Orwell*

You can't have a revolution unless you make it for
yourself; there is no such thing as a benevolent
dictatorship.

ibid.

The problem for the world as a whole is not how to
distribute such wealth as exists but how to increase
production, without which economic equality merely
means common misery.

Collected Essays, Journalism and Letters, vol. 4

I had come here to shoot at 'Fascists'; but a man who is holding up his trousers isn't a 'Fascist', he is visibly a fellow creature, similar to yourself, and you don't feel like shooting at him.

ibid., vol. 2

It is usual to speak of the Fascist objective as the 'beehive state', which does a grave injustice to bees. A world of rabbits ruled by stoats would be nearer the mark.

The Road to Wigan Pier

Socialism

One would get into trouble in left-wing circles for saying so, but the feeling of many Socialists towards their party is very similar to that of the thicker-headed type of public-school man towards his old school.

Collected Essays, Journalism and Letters, vol. 1

So much of left-wing thought is a kind of playing with fire by people who don't even know that fire is hot.

ibid.

Above a certain point – which should bear a fixed relation to the lowest current wage – all incomes should be taxed out of existence.

ibid., vol. 3

Particularly on the Left, political thought is a sort of masturbation fantasy in which the world of facts hardly matters.

ibid.

The typical Socialist ... a prim little man with a white-collar job, usually a secret teetotaller and often with vegetarian leanings.

The Road to Wigan Pier

As with the Christian religion, the worst advertisement for Socialism is its adherents.

ibid.

In order that Hitler may march the goose-step, that the Pope may denounce Bolshevism, that the cricket crowds may assemble at Lord's, that the Nancy poets may scratch one another's backs, coal has got to be forthcoming.

ibid.

It is only because miners sweat their guts out that superior persons can remain superior.

ibid.

One sometimes gets the impression that the mere words 'Socialism' and 'Communism' draw towards them with magnetic force every fruit-juice drinker, nudist, sandal-wearer, sex-maniac, Quaker, 'Nature Cure' quack, pacifist, and feminist in England.

ibid.

Socialism means justice and common decency ... The essential aims of Socialism are justice and liberty.

ibid.

The Socialist who finds his children playing with soldiers is usually upset, but he is never able to think of a substitute for the tin soldiers; tin pacifists somehow won't do.

Collected Essays, Journalism and Letters, vol. 2

The struggle of the working class is like the growth of a plant. The plant is blind and stupid, but it knows enough to keep pushing towards the light.

ibid.

The thing that attracts ordinary men to Socialism and makes them willing to risk their skins for it, the 'mystique' of Socialism, is the idea of equality; to the vast majority of people Socialism means a classless society, or it means nothing at all.

Homage to Catalonia

If there is hope ... it lies with the proles.

Nineteen Eighty-Four

One sees only the struggle of the gradually awakening common people against the lords of property and their hired liars and bumsuckers.

Homage to Catalonia

Every intelligent boy of sixteen is a Socialist. At that age one does not see the hook sticking out of the rather stodgy bait.

Keep the Aspidistra Flying

Imperialism

The real quarrel of the Fascist powers with British imperialism is that they know it is disintegrating.
The Lion and the Unicorn

The Empire was peaceful as no area of comparable size has ever been.

ibid.

In any town in India the European Club is the spiritual citadel, the real seat of British power, the Nirvana for which native officials and millionaires pine in vain.
Burmese Days

Most people can be at ease in a foreign country only when they are disparaging the local inhabitants.

ibid.

In India, do as the English do.

ibid.

With one part of my mind I thought of the British Raj as an unbreakable tyranny ... with another part I thought that the greatest joy in the world would be to drive a bayonet into a Buddhist priest's guts.
Collected Essays, Journalism and Letters, vol. 1

When the white man turns tyrant it is his own freedom that he destroys. He becomes a sort of hollow, posing dummy, the conventionalized figure of a sahib ... He wears a mask, and his face grows to fit it.

ibid.

A white man mustn't be frightened in front of 'natives'; and so, in general, he isn't frightened.

ibid.

In order to hate imperialism you have got to be a part of it.
                                                    The Road to Wigan Pier

The truth is that no modern man, in his heart of hearts, believes that it is right to invade a foreign country and hold the population down by force.
                                                    ibid.

Under the capitalist system, in order that England may live in comparative comfort, a hundred million Indians must live on the verge of starvation ... The alternative is to throw the Empire overboard and reduce England to a cold and unimportant little island where we should all have to work very hard and live mainly on herrings and potatoes.
                                                    ibid.

We're not civilizing them, we're only rubbing our dirt on to them.
                                                    Burmese Days

Orientals can be very provoking.
                                                    The Road to Wigan Pier

People with brown skins are next door to invisible.
                          Collected Essays, Journalism and Letters, vol. 1

I know enough of British imperialism not to like it, but I would support it against Nazism or Japanese imperialism, as a lesser evil.
                                                    ibid., vol. 3

Where the Japanese found themselves faced with the problem of ruling over a people more primitive than themselves, they dealt with it by simply wiping the aboriginal inhabitants out.
                                    George Orwell: The War Commentaries

To the coloured races they [the Germans] promise liberty, and simultaneously they appeal to the white races to combine for the exploitation of the coloured races.
                                                    ibid.

It is only when you meet someone of a different culture from yourself that you begin to realize what your own beliefs really are.

The Road to Wigan Pier

My whole life, every white man's life in the East, was one long struggle not to be laughed at.

Collected Essays, Journalism and Letters, vol. 1

Women

The Woman Business! What a bore it is! What a pity we can't cut it right out, or at least be like the animals – minutes of ferocious lust and months of icy chastity.
Keep the Aspidistra Flying

How many women really end up on the streets? A damn sight more end up at the mangle.
Coming Up For Air

I've come home from work, I've lain on my bed with all my clothes on except my shoes, wondering about women. Why they're like that, how they get like that, whether they're doing it on purpose.
ibid.

She was just pretty enough, and just plain enough, to be the kind of girl that men habitually pester.
A Clergyman's Daughter

A woman cannot be low without being disgusting, whereas a good male comedian can give the impression of something irredeemable and yet innocent.
Collected Essays, Journalism and Letters, vol. 2

One of the surest signs of his [Conrad's] genius is that women dislike his books.
ibid., vol. 1

Intelligent women are very rare animals, and if one wants to marry a woman who is intelligent *and* pretty, then the choice is still further restricted.
ibid., vol. 4

One of the big failures in human history has been the age-long attempt to stop women painting their faces.
ibid., vol. 3

The worst insult to a woman, either in London or in Paris, is 'cow'; a name which might even be a compliment, for cows are among the most likeable of animals.

Down and Out in Paris and London

'You're only a rebel from the waist downwards,' he told her.

Nineteen Eighty-Four

The woman down there had no mind, she had only strong arms, a warm heart, and a fertile belly.

ibid.

Famous People

Karl Marx
Literally a prophet, a tipster who not only tells you which horse to back, but also provides the reason why the horse didn't win.

Collected Essays, Journalism and Letters, vol. 1

Sir Oswald Mosley
One would have had to look a long time to find a man more barren of ideas than Sir Oswald Mosley. He is as hollow as a jug.

The Lion and the Unicorn

Henrik Ibsen
Ibsen, who left me with a vague impression that in Norway it's always raining.

Coming Up For Air

Stanley Baldwin
One could not even dignify him with the name of stuffed shirt. He was simply a hole in the air.

The Lion and the Unicorn

Neville Chamberlain
He was merely a stupid old man doing his best according to his very dim lights.

Collected Essays, Journalism and Letters, vol. 2

Clement Attlee
Attlee reminds me of nothing so much as a recently dead fish, before it has had time to stiffen.

ibid.

H.G. Wells
The minds of all of us, and therefore the physical world, would be perceptibly different if Wells had never existed.

ibid.

Is it not a sort of parricide for a person of my age ... to find fault with H.G. Wells?

ibid.

George Bernard Shaw
The basis of all Bernard Shaw's attacks on Shakespeare is really the charge – quite true, of course – that Shakespeare wasn't an enlightened member of the Fabian Society.

ibid.

Adolf Hitler
I have reflected that I would certainly kill him if I could get within reach of him, but that I could feel no personal animosity. The fact is that there is something deeply appealing about him.

ibid.

Rudyard Kipling
I worshipped Kipling at thirteen, loathed him at seventeen, enjoyed him at twenty, despised him at twenty-five, and now again rather admire him.

ibid., vol. 1

W.H. Auden
A sort of gutless Kipling.

The Road to Wigan Pier

Salvador Dali
A good draughtsman and a disgusting human being.
Collected Essays, Journalism and Letters, vol. 3

Jean-Paul Sartre
A bag of wind.

ibid., vol. 4

Mahatma Gandhi
Regarded simply as a politician, and compared with other leading political figures of our times, how clean a smell he has managed to leave behind!

ibid.

Jonathan Swift
Swift did not possess ordinary wisdom, but he did
possess a terrible intensity of vision, capable of picking
out a single hidden truth and then magnifying it and
distorting it.

ibid.

Malcolm Muggeridge
He is looking only on the black side, but it is doubtful
whether there is any bright side to look on.

ibid., vol. 1

Charles Dickens
A man who is always fighting against something, but
who fights in the open and is not frightened ... a man
who is *generously angry*.

ibid.

Bertrand Russell
So long as he and a few others like him are alive and out
of jail, we know that the world is still sane in parts ... He
has an essentially *decent* intellect, a kind of intellectual
chivalry which is far rarer than mere cleverness.

ibid.

T.S. Eliot
... achieve[s] the difficult feat of making modern life out
to be worse than it is.

ibid.

Joseph Stalin
[July 1941] This disgusting murderer is temporarily on
our side.

ibid., vol. 2

Himself

This age makes me so sick that sometimes I am almost impelled to stop at a corner and start calling down curses from Heaven like Jeremiah or Ezra or somebody.
Collected Essays, Journalism and Letters, vol. 1

So long as I remain alive and well I shall continue to feel strongly about prose style, to love the surface of the earth, and to take pleasure in solid objects and scraps of useless information.

ibid.

I have been fighting for years against the systematic faking of history which now goes on.

ibid., vol. 3

My starting point is always a feeling of partisanship, a sense of injustice.

ibid., vol. 1

I hold the outmoded opinion that in the long run it does not pay to tell lies.

ibid.

Outside my work the thing I care about most is gardening, especially vegetable gardening.

ibid., vol. 2

I watched a man hanged once; it seemed to me worse than a hundred murders. I never went into a jail without feeling ... that my place was on the other side of the bars.
The Road to Wigan Pier

Looking back upon that period, I seem to have spent half the time in denouncing the capitalist system and the other half raging over the insolence of bus-conductors.

ibid.

At that time failure seemed to me to be the only virtue. Every suspicion of self-advancement ... seemed to me spiritually ugly, a species of bullying.

ibid.

I am a degenerate modern semi-intellectual who would die if I did not get my early morning cup of tea and my *New Statesman* every Friday. *ibid.*

From the age of eight, or even earlier, the consciousness of sin was never far away from me.

Collected Essays, Journalism and Letters, vol. 4

With me, when I am drunk, my brain remains clear long after my legs and speech have gone.

ibid., vol. 1

It took me thirty years to work off the effects of being called Eric. *ibid.*, vol. 2

I am rather glad to have been hit by a bullet because I think it will happen to us all in the near future and I am glad to know it doesn't hurt.

ibid., vol. 1

I am afraid I definitely lack glamour. *ibid.*, vol. 2

Every line of serious work that I have written since 1936 has been written, directly or indirectly, *against* totalitarianism and *for* democratic Socialism, as I understand it.

ibid., vol. 1

I see that it is invariably where I lacked a *political* purpose that I wrote lifeless books, and was betrayed into purple passages, sentences without meaning, decorative adjectives and humbug generally.

ibid.

There has literally been not one day in which I did not feel that I was idling ... I have never been able to get away from this neurotic feeling that I was wasting time.
ibid., vol. 4

I knew that I had a facility with words and a power of facing unpleasant facts.

ibid., vol. 1

I want a civilization in which 'progress' is not definable as making the world safe for little fat men.

The Road to Wigan Pier

All my life I had sworn that I would not duck the first time a bullet passed over me; but the movement appears to be instinctive, and almost everybody does it at least once.

Homage to Catalonia

In theory I rather admire the Spaniards for not sharing our Northern time-neurosis; but unfortunately I share it myself.

ibid.

Language, Literature & Art

Good prose is like a window pane.
Collected Essays, Journalism and Letters, vol. 1

Writing a book is a horrible, exhausting struggle, like a long bout of some painful illness. One would never undertake such a thing if one were not driven on by some demon whom one can neither resist nor understand. *ibid.*

Never start writing novels, if you wish to preserve your happiness. *ibid.*

The worst thing one can do with words is surrender to them.
ibid., vol. 4

In a grocer's shop people come in to buy something, in a bookshop they come in to make a nuisance of themselves.
ibid., vol. 1

Language ought to be the joint creation of poets and manual workers.
ibid., vol. 3

The best books … are those that tell you what you know already.
Nineteen Eighty-Four

Even to want to write about so-called artists who spend on sodomy what they have gained by sponging betrays a kind of spiritual inadequacy.
Collected Essays, Journalism and Letters, vol. 1

All art is propaganda … On the other hand, not all propaganda is art.
ibid.

It is fatal for the caricaturist to see too much.

ibid.

Poetry on the air sounds like the Muses in striped
trousers.

ibid., vol. 2

There are no rules in novel writing, and for any work of
art there is only one test worth bothering about –
survival.

ibid., vol. 1

It is an unusual novel that does not contain somewhere
or other a portrait of the author, thinly disguised as hero,
saint or martyr.

ibid., vol. 4

I have three more chapters and an epilogue to do, and
then I shall spend about two months putting on the
twiddly bits.

ibid., vol. 1

What people always demand of a popular novelist is
that he shall write the same book over and over again,
forgetting that a man who would write the same book
twice could not even write it once.

ibid.

When one reads any strongly individual piece of
writing, one has the impression of seeing a face
somewhere behind the page. It is not necessarily the
actual face of the writer.

ibid.

All fiction … is censored in the interests of the ruling
class.

ibid.

The novel is practically a Protestant form of art; it is a
product of the free mind, of the autonomous individual.

ibid.

The great enemy of clear language is insincerity. When there is a gap between one's real and one's declared aims, one turns as it were instinctively to long words and exhausted idioms, like a cuttlefish squirting out ink ... But if thought corrupts language, language can corrupt thought.
ibid., vol. 4

In our time, political speech and writing are largely the defence of the indefensible.
ibid.

If a writer on a political subject manages to preserve a detached attitude, it is nearly always because he does not know what he is talking about. To understand a political movement one has got to be involved in it, and as soon as one is involved one becomes a propagandist.
ibid., vol. 1

Let the meaning choose the word, and not the other way about.
ibid., vol. 4

One can cure oneself of the *not un-* formation by memorizing this sentence: A not unblack dog was chasing a not unsmall rabbit across a not ungreen field.
ibid.

It is questionable whether anyone who has had long experience as a free-lance journalist ought to become an editor. It is too like taking a convict out of his cell and making him governor of the prison.
ibid.

Whoever writes of his childhood must beware of exaggeration and self-pity.
ibid.

The mere sound of words ending in –ism seems to bring with it the smell of propaganda.
ibid.

Innumerable controversial books ... are judged before they are read, and in effect before they are written.
ibid.

It is not easy for most modern writers to imagine the mental processes of anyone who is not a writer.

ibid.

I really think that this modern habit of describing love-making in detail is something that future generations will look back on as we do on things like the death of Little Nell.

ibid.

Philosophy should be forbidden by law.

ibid.

The modern English literary world, at any rate the highbrow section of it, is a sort of poisonous jungle where only weeds can flourish.

The Road to Wigan Pier

The worst thing we can say about a work of art is that it is insincere.

Collected Essays, Journalism and Letters, vol. 2

There is only one way to make money at writing and that is to marry a publisher's daughter.

Down and Out in Paris and London

For sheer dirtiness of fighting, the feud between the inventors of the international languages would take a lot of beating.

Collected Essays, Journalism and Letters, vol. 4

Of all types of human being, only the artist takes it upon himself to say that he 'cannot' work.

Keep the Aspidistra Flying

If you had to define humour in a single phrase, you might define it as dignity sitting on a tin-tack.

Collected Essays, Journalism and Letters, vol. 3

Whatever is funny is subversive, every joke is ultimately a custard pie ... A dirty joke ... is a sort of mental revolution.

ibid., vol. 2

For my part I don't object to old jokes – indeed, I reverence them. When sea-sickness and adultery have ceased to be funny, western civilization will have ceased to exist.   *ibid.*, vol. 1

I think that the idea of the deliberate invention of words is at least worth thinking over.

ibid., vol. 2

Don't you see that the whole aim of Newspeak is to narrow the range of thought? In the end we shall make thoughtcrime literally impossible, because there will be no words in which to express it.

Nineteen Eighty-Four

Every year fewer and fewer words, and the range of consciousness always a little smaller.

ibid.

To wear an improper expression on your face (to look incredulous when a victory was announced, for example) was itself a punishable offence. There was even a word for it: *facecrime* it was called.

ibid.

To do anything that suggested a taste for solitude, even to go for a walk by yourself, was always slightly dangerous. There was a word for it in Newspeak: *ownlife*, it was called, meaning individualism and eccentricity.   *ibid.*

Ultimately it was hoped to make articulate speech issue from the larynx without involving the higher brain centres at all. This aim was frankly admitted in the Newspeak word *duckspeak*.   *ibid.*

Oldthinkers unbellyfeel Ingsoc.

ibid.

Snooty, refined books on safe painters and safe poets by those moneyed young beasts who glide so gracefully from Eton to Cambridge and from Cambridge to the literary reviews.   *Keep the Aspidistra Flying*

Wherever there is enforced orthodoxy – or even two orthodoxies, as often happens – good writing stops.

Collected Essays, Journalism and Letters, vol. 4

Political writing in our time consists almost entirely of prefabricated phrases bolted together like the pieces of a child's Meccano set.

ibid.

To write in plain, vigorous language one has to think fearlessly, and if one thinks fearlessly one cannot be politically orthodox.

ibid.

[6th rule for writing good prose] Break any of these rules sooner than say anything outright barbarous.

ibid.

Education

Probably the greatest cruelty one can inflict on a child is to send it to school among children richer than itself. A child conscious of poverty will suffer snobbish agonies such as a grown-up person can scarcely even imagine.
Keep the Aspidistra Flying

He was a liar and a footballer, the two things absolutely necessary for success at school. *Burmese Days*

A middle-class child is taught almost simultaneously to wash his neck, to be ready to die for his country, and to despise the 'lower classes'.

The Road to Wigan Pier

You forget your Latin and Greek within a few months of leaving school ... but your snobbishness, unless you persistently root it out like the bindweed it is, sticks by you till your grave. *ibid.*

I've always held that the public schools aren't so bad, but people are wrecked by those filthy private schools long before they get to public school age.
Collected Essays, Journalism and Letters, vol. 1

Only by resurrecting our own memories can we realize how incredibly distorted is the child's vision of the world.

ibid., vol. 4

Look back into your own childhood and think of the nonsense you used to believe. *ibid.*

'Cultured' middle-class life has reached a depth of softness at which a public-school education – five years in a lukewarm bath of snobbery – can actually be looked back upon as an eventful period.

ibid., vol. 1

History

If the Party could thrust its hand into the past and say of
this or that event, it never happened – that, surely was
more terrifying that mere torture and death?

Nineteen Eighty-Four

All history was a palimpsest, scraped clean and
reinscribed as often as was necessary.

ibid.

'Who controls the past,' ran the Party slogan, 'controls
the future: who controls the present controls the past.'

ibid.

Day by day and almost minute by minute the past was
brought up to date.

ibid.

He accepted everything. The past was alterable. The past
never had been altered.

ibid.

Contrary to popular belief, the past was not more
eventful than the present.

Collected Essays, Journalism and Letters, vol. 1

History is written by the winners.

ibid., vol. 3

Nations do not escape from their past merely by making
a revolution.

The Lion and the Unicorn

A history constructed imaginatively would never be
right about any single event, but it might come nearer to
essential truth than a mere compilation of names and dates
in which no one statement was demonstrably untrue.

Collected Essays, Journalism and Letters, vol. 4

History consists of a series of swindles, in which the masses are first lured into revolt by the promise of utopia, and then, when they have done their job, enslaved over again by new masters.

ibid.

History stopped in 1936.

ibid., vol. 1

I am willing to believe that history is for the most part inaccurate and biased, but what is peculiar to our own age is the abandonment of the idea that history *could* be truthfully written.

ibid.

Pessimism

The only 'ism' that has ever justified itself is pessimism.
Collected Essays, Journalism and Letters, vol. 1

When one does get some credit in this life, it is usually for something one has not done.
Burmese Days

Oughtn't to prefer trees to men? I say it depends what trees and what men.
Coming Up For Air

Isn't it queer how we go through life, always thinking that the things we want to do are the things that can't be done? *ibid.*

Wherever we're going, we're going downwards. Into the grave, into the cesspool – no knowing ... There's something that's gone out of us in these twenty years since the war. It's a kind of vital juice that we've squirted away until there's nothing left.
ibid.

They say that happy people have no histories, and neither do the blokes who work in insurance offices.
ibid.

There is a humility about genuine love that is rather horrible in some ways.
Burmese Days

Kids are a 'link', as they say. Or a 'tie'. Not to say a ball and fetter.
Coming Up For Air

Why is it that one can't borrow from a rich friend but can from a half-starved relative?
Keep the Aspidistra Flying

If our methods of making war had kept pace with our methods of keeping house, we should be just about on the verge of discovering gunpowder.

Collected Essays, Journalism and Letters, vol. 3

We are all drowning in filth ... All power is in the hands of paranoiacs. *ibid.,* vol. 2

This is the twilight of Parliamentary democracy and these creatures are simply ghosts gibbering in some corner while the real events happen elsewhere.

ibid.

That seems to be a fixed rule in London: whenever you do by some chance have a decent vista, block it up with the ugliest statue you can find.

ibid., vol. 3

Hedonistic societies do not endure.

ibid., vol. 2

The attempt to cling to youth at all costs, to attempt to preserve your sexual attraction, to see even in middle age a future for yourself and not merely for your children, is a thing of recent growth and has only precariously established itself. It will probably disappear again. *ibid.*

Modern man is rather like a bisected wasp which goes on sucking jam and pretends that the loss of its abdomen does not matter.

ibid., vol. 1

Man is not a Yahoo, but he is rather like a Yahoo and needs to be reminded of it from time to time.

ibid.

Getting and spending we lay waste our powers.

ibid.

In order to rule over barbarians, you have got to become a barbarian yourself.

ibid.

Coming up for air! But there isn't any air. The dustbin that we're in reaches up to the stratosphere.

Coming Up For Air

I don't know what you ought to feel, but I'll tell you what I did feel, and that was nothing.

ibid.

In a town like London there are always plenty of not quite certifiable lunatics walking the streets.

Collected Essays, Journalism and Letters, vol. 1

Consider how fatally easy it is to get married.

ibid., vol. 3

If there is a wrong thing to do, it will be done, infallibly. One has come to believe in that as if it were a law of nature.

ibid., vol. 2

Serious sport has nothing to do with fair play. It is bound up with hatred, jealousy, boastfulness, disregard of all rules and sadistic pleasure in witnessing violence: in other words it is war minus the shooting.

ibid., vol. 4

Much of what goes by the name of pleasure is simply an effort to destroy consciousness.

ibid.

To see what is in front of one's nose needs a constant struggle.

ibid.

In general, one is only right when either wish or fear coincides with reality.

ibid.

Every February since 1940 I have found myself thinking that this time winter is going to be permanent.

ibid.

People talk about the horrors of war, but what weapon has a man invented that even approaches in cruelty some of the commoner diseases? 'Natural' death, almost by definition, means something slow, smelly and painful.

ibid.

If I were a bookmaker, simply calculating the probabilities and leaving my own wishes out of account, I would give odds against the survival of civilization within the next few hundred years.

ibid.

Most people get a fair amount of fun out of their lives, but on balance life is suffering, and only the very young or the very foolish imagine otherwise.

ibid.

The aim of a joke is not to degrade the human being but to remind him that he is already degraded.

ibid., vol. 3

When you are on a sinking ship, your thoughts will be about sinking ships.

ibid., vol. 4

The fact is that human beings only started fighting one another in earnest when there was no longer anything to fight about.

ibid.

There is a great deal of inherent sadness and loneliness in human life that would be the same whatever the circumstances.

ibid.

At 50, everyone has the face he deserves.

ibid.

In a crowded, dirty little country like ours one takes defilement almost for granted.

The Road to Wigan Pier

We may find in the long run that tinned food is a deadlier weapon than the machine gun.

ibid.

The English palate, especially the working-class palate, now rejects good food almost automatically.

ibid.

You can have an affection for a murderer or a sodomite, but you cannot have an affection for a man whose breath stinks.

ibid.

Snobbishness is one of those vices which we can discern in everyone else but never in ourselves.

ibid.

This is the inevitable fate of the sentimentalist. All his opinions change into their opposites at the first brush of reality.

ibid.

Is not anyone with any degree of mental honesty conscious of telling lies all day long, both in talking and writing, simply because lies will fall into artistic shape when truth will not?

Collected Essays, Journalism and Letters, vol. 2

The choice before human beings is not, as a rule, between good and evil but between two evils.

ibid.

A humanitarian is always a hypocrite.

ibid.

I never thought I should grow blasé about the sound of gunfire, but so I have.

ibid.

[The BBC] What a mixture of whoreshop and lunatic asylum it is for the most part.

ibid.

They say no English hops ever go into beer nowadays, they're all made into chemicals. Chemicals, on the other hand, are made into beer.

Coming Up For Air

We live in a lunatic world in which opposites are constantly changing into one another, in which pacifists find themselves worshipping Hitler, Socialists become nationalists, patriots become quislings, Buddhists pray for the success of the Japanese army, and the Stock Market takes an upward turn when the Russians stage an offensive.

Collected Essays, Journalism and Letters, vol. 2

A world in which it is wrong to murder an individual civilian and right to drop a thousand tons of high explosives on a residential area does sometimes make me wonder whether this earth of ours is not a loony-bin made use of by some other planet.

ibid., vol. 3

Autobiography is only to be trusted when it reveals something disgraceful.

ibid.

Like a drug, the machine is useful, dangerous, and habit-forming. The oftener one surrenders to it the tighter its grip becomes.

The Road to Wigan Pier

The truth is that many of the qualities we admire in human beings can only function in opposition to some kind of disaster, pain, or difficulty.

ibid.

The logical end of mechanical progress is to reduce the human being to something resembling a brain in a bottle.

ibid.

The food crank is by definition a person willing to cut himself off from human society in hopes of adding five years on to the life of his carcase.

ibid.

I have noticed that people who let lodgings nearly always hate their lodgers.

ibid.

Early in life I noticed that no event is ever correctly reported in a newspaper.
Collected Essays, Journalism and Letters, vol. 1

When human beings are governed by 'thou shalt not', the individual can practise a certain amount of eccentricity: when they are supposedly governed by 'love' or 'reason', he is under continuous pressure to make him behave and think in exactly the same way as everyone else.

ibid., vol. 4

He had reached the age when the future ceases to be a rosy blur and becomes actual and menacing.
Keep the Aspidistra Flying

There is nothing more dreadful in the world than to live in somebody else's house, eating his bread and doing nothing in return for it.

ibid.

However delicately it is disguised, charity is still horrible; there is a malaise, almost a secret hatred, between the giver and the receiver.

ibid.

There is no emotion that matters greatly when one is standing at a street corner in a biting wind.

ibid.

One of the effects of safe and civilized life is an immense oversensitiveness which makes all the primary emotions seem somewhat disgusting. Generosity is as painful as meanness, gratitude as hateful as ingratitude.
Collected Essays, Journalism and Letters, vol. 2

Let a certain note be struck, let this or that corn be trodden on ... and the most fair-minded and sweet-tempered person may suddenly be transformed into a vicious partisan, anxious only to 'score' over his adversary and indifferent as to how many lies he tells or how many logical errors he commits in doing so.

ibid., vol. 3

Tragedy, he perceived, belonged to the ancient time, to a
time when there was still privacy, love, and friendship,
and when the members of a family stood by one another
without needing to know the reason.

Nineteen Eighty-Four

Nothing was your own except the few cubic centimetres
inside your skull.

ibid.

If you want a picture of the future, imagine a boot
stamping on a human face – for ever.

ibid.

If you want to keep a secret you must also hide it from
yourself.

ibid.

The thing that is in Room 101 is the worst thing in the
world.

ibid.

He loved Big Brother.

ibid.

I wasn't born for an age like this;
Was Smith? Was Jones? Were you?

Collected Essays, Journalism and Letters, vol. 1

Blessed are they who are stricken only with classifiable
diseases.

Burmese Days

Those who take the sword perish by the sword, and
those who don't take the sword perish by smelly
diseases.

Collected Essays, Journalism and Letters, vol. 4

Optimism

What I felt was something that's so unusual nowadays that to say it sounds like foolishness. I felt happy. I felt that though I shan't live for ever, I'd be quite ready to.
Coming Up for Air

When it comes to the pinch, human beings are heroic.
Collected Essays, Journalism and Letters, vol. 2

So long as comedians like Max Miller are on the stage and the comic coloured postcards which express approximately the same view of life are in the stationers' windows, one knows that the popular culture of England is surviving.
ibid.

On the whole, human beings want to be good, but not too good and not quite all the time.
ibid.

Perhaps when the pinch comes the common people will turn out to be more intelligent than the clever ones. I certainly hope so.
ibid., vol. 1

To raise the standard of living of the whole world to that of Britain would not be a greater undertaking than the war we have just fought.
Homage to Catalonia

The planting of a tree, especially one of the long-living hardwood trees, is a gift which you can make to posterity at almost no cost and with almost no trouble, and if the tree takes root it will far outlive the visible effects of any of your other actions, good or evil.
Collected Essays, Journalism and Letters, vol. 4

Above the level of a third- or fourth-grade moron, life has got to be lived largely in terms of effort.
The Road to Wigan Pier

Conscious futility is something only for the young ...
Sooner or later one is obliged to adopt a positive attitude
towards life and society.

Collected Essays, Journalism and Letters, vol. 2

Has it ever struck you that there's a thin man inside
every fat man, just as there's a statue inside every block
of stone?

Coming Up For Air

Before the war, and especially before the Boer War, it
was summer all year round.

ibid.

Actually you can only love your enemies if you are
willing to kill them in certain circumstances.

Collected Essays, Journalism and Letters, vol. 2

It is a great thing to die in your bed, though it is better
still to die in your boots.

ibid., vol. 4

I think that by retaining one's childhood love of such
things as trees, fishes, butterflies and ... toads, one
makes a peaceful and decent future a little more
probable.

ibid.

I can respect anyone who is willing to face unpopularity.

ibid., vol. 3

There is no reason to think that the supposed acquisitive
instincts of the human being could not be bred out in a
couple of generations.

ibid.

So long as you are not actually ill, hungry, frightened or
immured in a prison or a holiday camp, spring is still
spring. The atom bombs are piling up in the factories,
the police are prowling through the cities, the lies are
streaming from the loudspeakers, but the earth is still
going round the sun, and neither the dictators nor the
bureaucrats, deeply as they disapprove of the process,
are able to prevent it.

ibid., vol. 4

Snobbishness, like hypocrisy, is a check upon behaviour whose value from a social point of view has been underrated.

ibid., vol. 3

How can you call yourself a tea-lover if you destroy the flavour of your tea by putting sugar in it?

ibid.

The fact to which we have got to cling, as to a life-belt, is that it *is* possible to be a normal decent person and yet to be fully alive.

ibid., vol. 1

Freedom is the freedom to say that two plus two make four. If that is granted, all else follows.

Nineteen Eighty-Four

To an ordinary human being, love means nothing if it does not mean loving some people more than others.

Collected Essays, Journalism and Letters, vol. 4

No decent person cares tuppence for the opinion of posterity.

ibid., vol. 3

Talent, which is probably another name for conviction.

ibid., vol. 4

Why don't people, instead of the idiocies they do spend their time on, just walk round *looking* at things?

Coming Up For Air

The essence of being human is that one does not seek perfection, that one *is* sometimes willing to commit sins for the sake of loyalty, that one does not push asceticism to the point where it makes friendly intercourse impossible, and that one is prepared in the end to be defeated and broken up by life, which is the inevitable price of fastening one's loyalties upon other human individuals.

Collected Essays, Journalism and Letters, vol. 4

Man only stays human by preserving large patches of simplicity in his life.

ibid.

When I saw the prisoner step aside to avoid the puddle, I saw … the unspeakable wrongness of cutting a life short when it is in full tide … and in two minutes, with a sudden snap, one of us would be gone – one mind less, one world less.

ibid., vol. 1

Man is not … a kind of walking stomach; he has also got a hand, an eye, and a brain. Cease to use your hands, and you have lopped off a huge chunk of your consciousness.

The Road to Wigan Pier

Really vital people … multiply almost as automatically as animals.

Keep the Aspidistra Flying

Revenge is an act which you want to commit when you are powerless and because you are powerless: as soon as the sense of impotence is removed, the desire evaporates also.

Collected Essays, Journalism and Letters, vol. 4